Coffee Talk: Project Special Day

A Parent & Child's Activity Guide for Building Memorable Moments

Tyler Hayden
&
Breton Hayden

Tyler Hayden Inc.
Lunenburg, Nova Scotia, Canada

Coffee Talk Series
www.tylerhayden.com

Published by Tyler Hayden
Box 1112
Lunenburg, Nova Scotia
B0J 2C0

Editor: Paula Sarson

Cover & Page Design: Kathryn Marcellino
Printed and bound in USA

National Library of Canada Cataloguing in Publication

Hayden, Tyler, 1974- and Hayden, Breton, 2007-
Coffee Talk: Project Special Day, A Parent & Child's Activity Guide for Building Memorable Moments

ISBN-13: 978-1-897050-20-0

1. Parenting. 2. Family. 3. Games. I. Title.

This book is dedicated to you. Thank you for taking a few moments from your busy schedule to truly make an impact on someone you love.

"We Don't Remember Days, We Remember Moments."

You could say the way Breton and Tyler hit the road together is a bit...different. They love to hang out, and it doesn't really matter what they do. It could be grocery shopping, playing with dolls in the toy aisle of a department store, or trekking through a park to feed the ducks. The world is their oyster, and they love to make that oyster shine!

This father-and-daughter team holds double black belts in the "Art of the Special Day." They truly believe what the little plaque says on Breton's great-nanny's bathroom wall: "We don't remember days, we remember moments." This little sign's tattered patina relays a message that has seemingly been delivered through the ages, again and again, the reminder that our journey through life is made of brief memories, and those brief memories enrich our life and shape our legacy.

With that knowledge in mind, Breton and Tyler embark regularly on trips together and have designed ways to make those trips' moments amazing. They believe no moment should be wasted. In fact, it should be maximized to its full potential. That's where this book comes in.

Breton and Tyler have put together three of their favorite games that will get you started on maxing-out your adventure. Some random fun things to do...if you and your teammate are up for an adventure! Here is a quick description of the games they have included for you to play.

Coffee Talk

Heading out for a drive, sitting at a coffee shop, or just hanging out on the deck, this game is a fun way to share great moments and personal understandings. The child takes the book first, flips to any page, and reads the parent the question marked "PARENTS." The parent answers the question. Then the parent asks the child the paired question labeled "KIDS." It's that simple. The play goes back and forth, until you run out of questions or time.

Would You Rather

Here is another great game to play when you are traveling about. It's one of Breton and Tyler's favs to play when they are driving. It's totally random fun, that's why they like it. Once you get the hang of it, they're sure you will come up with some of your own questions. Take turns going first. You can either just talk about the questions, if you're driving, or take a moment and jot some notes/draw pictures in the box beside the question, which will help you remember your random creative wisdom later on.

Dates on the GO!

Special days are especially fun. Breton and Tyler like to make their special days memorable by finding new places to explore and things to do. So here's the plan for Dates on the Go: randomly pick one of the activities listed below. Then just go do it; it's that simple. When you are finished, capture a memory about the cool thing you did by drawing a picture, writing poem, or jotting some notes in the space on the page. You can also share the experience by posting a photo or calling a friend and telling them about your day. Special days are as great to share as they are to make.

Coffee Talk

Heading out for a drive, sitting at a coffee shop, or just hanging out on the deck, this game is a fun way to share great moments and personal understandings. The child takes the book first, flips to any page, and reads the parent the question marked "PARENTS." The parent answers the question. Then the parent asks the child the paired question labeled "KIDS." It's that simple. The play goes back and forth, until you run out of questions or time.

KIDS: Questions for kids to answer. Parents pose these questions to your child.

PARENTS: Questions for parents to answer. Kids pose these questions to your parent.

KIDS: What's your favorite app to play?

PARENTS: What was your favorite toy to play with when you were growing up?

KIDS: What's the best toy of all time?

PARENTS: Who was your favorite teacher in school?

KIDS: What's your favorite thing to do in winter?

PARENTS: What did you like better as a kid, pizza or candy?

KIDS: If you could add one cool thing (slide, tree fort, etc.) to your room, what would it be?

PARENTS: Where did you hang out when you were my age?

KIDS: Who is your favorite friend to have a play date with?

PARENTS: Can you describe your room when you were growing up?

KIDS: When did you last catch someone picking their nose?

PARENTS: What did you dream about doing when you were my age?

KIDS: What games do you like to play at recess?

PARENTS: What scared you when you were a kid?

KIDS: What is the funniest thing that happened at school?

PARENTS: When did you get in really big trouble as a kid, and what did you do?

KIDS: What was one thing someone did for you that was really nice?

PARENTS: Where was your secret hiding place when you were a kid?

KIDS: What is the nicest thing you have ever done for someone else?

PARENTS: Who is your favorite Disney character?

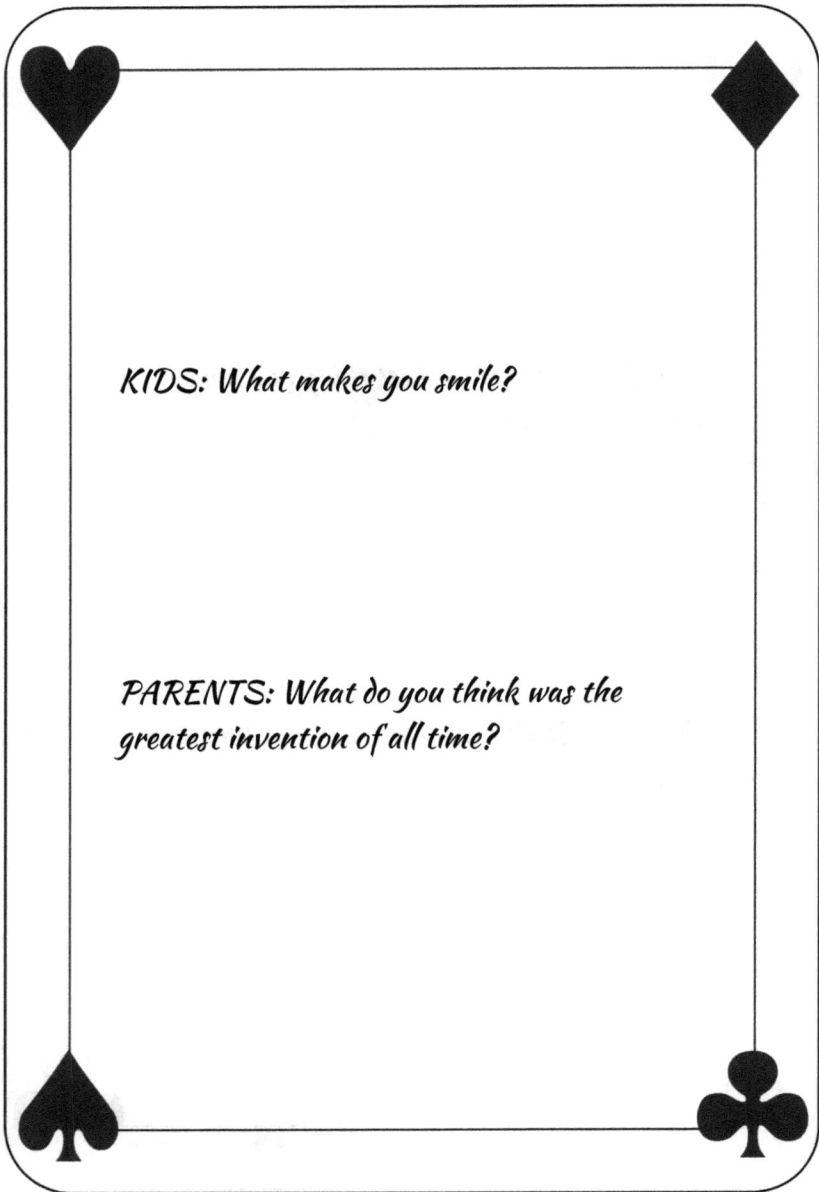

KIDS: What makes you smile?

PARENTS: What do you think was the greatest invention of all time?

KIDS: How should your teacher dress up for Halloween?

PARENTS: Who would win a battle: Superman or Spiderman, and why?

KIDS: What new thing did you learn today?

PARENTS: If you could have learned one thing as a kid that would have helped you as an adult, what would you have liked to learn more of?

KIDS: What is the hardest thing you've ever had to learn?

PARENTS: What was your favorite class and/or grade in school, and why?

KIDS: If you could go to one class all day, what one would it be, and why?

PARENTS: Where did you like to go shopping?

KIDS: If you could grow up to be just like one adult (other than your parents), who would it be?

PARENTS: Did you have a nickname as a kid?

KIDS: How do you know when someone is a good friend?

PARENTS: Who was the weirdest old person who lived near you and what was weird about them?

KIDS: If you could live inside one video game or movie for a day, which one would you like to live in?

PARENTS: Where was your most memorable travel destination as a kid?

KIDS: How do you know when someone is being a jerk?

PARENTS: What was your most embarrassing moment as a kid?

KIDS: What person do you know would survive a zombie apocalypse?

PARENTS: What was your favorite game to play as a kid?

KIDS: If you could eat one junk food all day long and never get sick, which one would it be?

PARENTS: Who was your best friend growing up, and why?

KIDS: Can you describe your life when you grow up?

PARENTS: What do you think I should be when I grow up?

29

KIDS: If you could travel to one place in the entire world for a week where would it be?

PARENTS: Can you show me on the Internet some of your favorite songs when you were in grade school?

KIDS: What is the best part about being a family pet?

PARENTS: What is your favorite movie?

KIDS: What is your favorite thing to do as a family?

PARENTS: What did you wear for PJs when you were my age?

KIDS: What store could you spend $1,000 in? And what would you buy?

PARENTS: Where did you like to go out to eat as a kid?

KIDS: What's your favorite movie of all time?

PARENTS: When were you most proud of yourself?

KIDS: What is one thing adults do that you think is weird?

PARENTS: What did you wish your name could have been, if you didn't have the one you have?

KIDS: What's your favorite thing to do that involves just me and you?

PARENTS: What was the coolest show, concert, or sporting event you went to?

KIDS: If you could own any car when you grow up, which one would you choose?

PARENTS: What's the coolest thing you ever found?

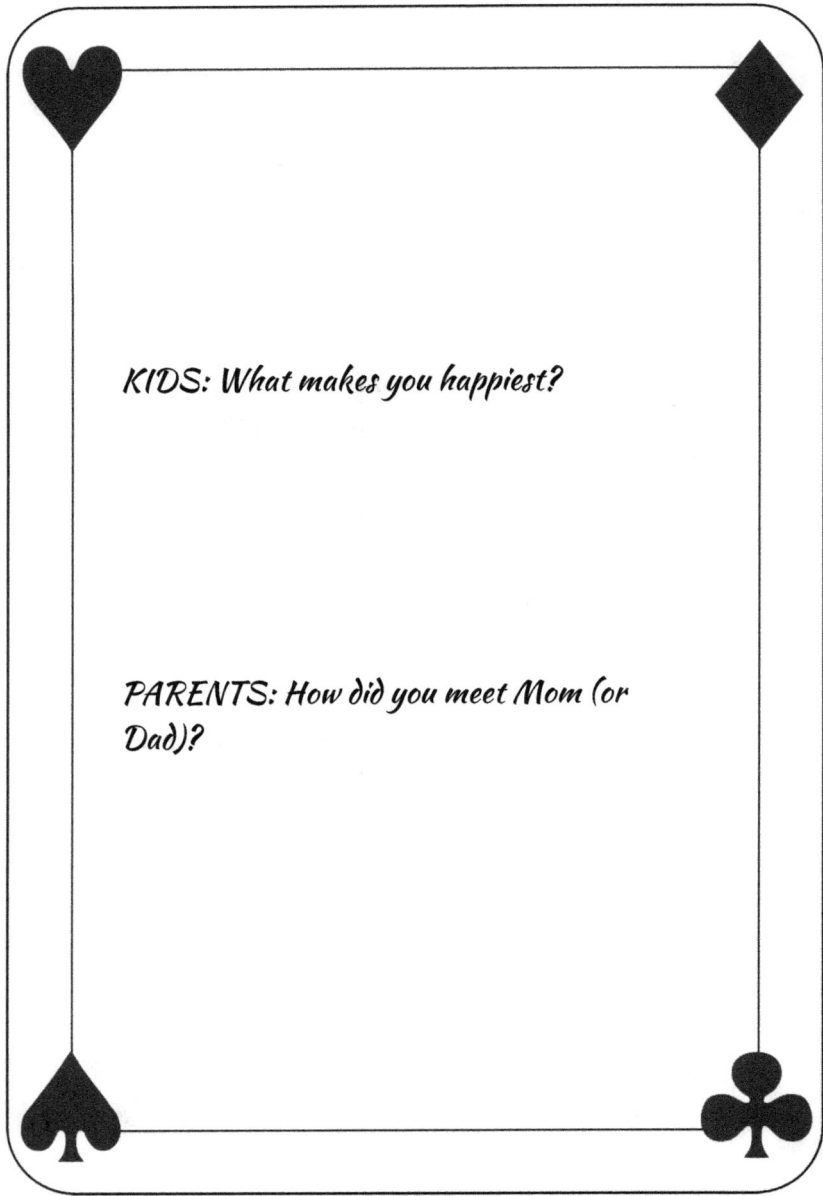

KIDS: What makes you happiest?

PARENTS: How did you meet Mom (or Dad)?

KIDS: If you could meet one music artist, who would it be?

PARENTS: Why was your Dad so cool?

KIDS: Why do you think parents drink so much coffee?

PARENTS: Why was your Mom so cool?

KIDS: What's the best sport on earth to play, and why?

PARENTS: What is one of your best vacation memories as a kid?

KIDS: What is one thing you would like to learn how to do?

PARENTS: What was your dream job when you were my age?

KIDS: What would be a really cool club to start?

PARENTS: What did you do after school with your friends?

KIDS: When you play by yourself, what's your favorite thing to do?

PARENTS: What was your favorite after-school snack?

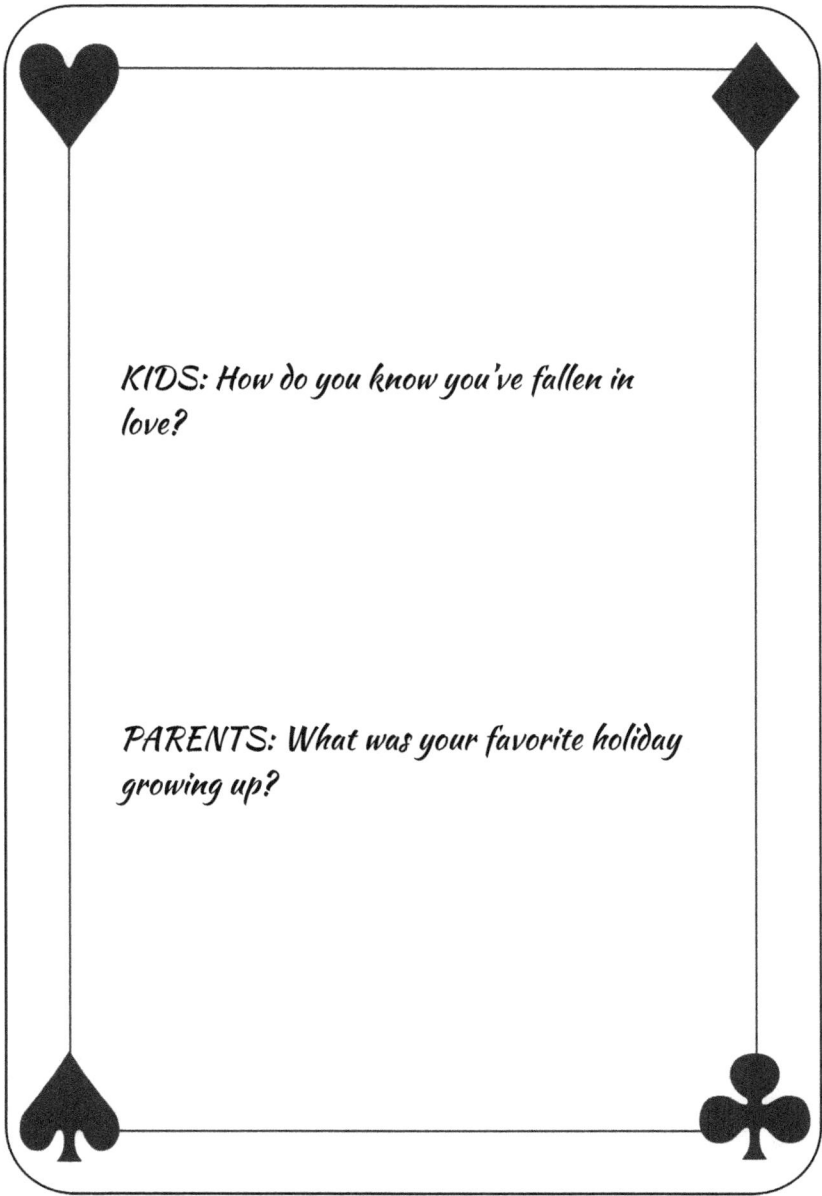

KIDS: How do you know you've fallen in love?

PARENTS: What was your favorite holiday growing up?

45

KIDS: Why do you like where we live?

PARENTS: What was the best birthday party you ever had? What happened?

KIDS: What's your favorite dinner to have as a family?

PARENTS: What was your favorite color growing up?

KIDS: Who would win in a wrestling match up: The Rock or Arnold Schwarzenegger?

PARENTS: What is one thing you wish you had done more of as a kid?

KIDS: What is your favorite toy to play with in the tub?

PARENTS: If you could eat one of these things forever, and never get sick or fat, what would you eat: pizza, ice cream, cookies, chocolate, burgers, or whipped cream?

KIDS: What is the biggest waste of time adults do?

PARENTS: If you could own any vehicle, what kind would you own?

KIDS: What famous actor/actress would you like to take a selfie with?

PARENTS: What was your first car?

KIDS: What was the best gift you ever received?

PARENTS: What do you like best about working?

KIDS: What are your goals right now?

PARENTS: Why did you choose the job you do?

KIDS: What was your favorite birthday party?

PARENTS: What was your favorite sport to play growing up?

Would You Rather

Here is another great game to play when you are traveling about. It's one of Breton and Tyler's favs to play when they are driving. It's totally random fun, that's why they like it. Once you get the hang of the game, they're sure you will come up with some of your own questions. Take turns going first. You can either just talk about the questions, if you're driving, or take a moment and jot some notes/draw pictures in the box beside the question, which will help you remember your random creative wisdom later on.

Would you rather eat at a fancy restaurant or a fast food restaurant?

Would you rather be a rainbow or a dark cloud?

Would you rather go dancing or have a campfire?

Would you rather be a house or a car?

Would you rather be a dog or a cat?

Would you rather eat ice cream or a cookie?

Would you rather go to your parents' workplace or your school for the day?

Would you rather wear a dress or a skirt?

Would you rather jump out of an airplane or swim with the sharks?

Would you rather camp in a campground or in the wilderness?

Would you rather be a firefighter or a police officer?

Would you rather be a vet or a doctor?

Would you rather have a chocolate lab or a poodle?

Would you rather drink coffee or tea?

Would you rather waterski or snow ski?

Would you rather sleep in or get up early?

Would you rather live on the beaches of Hawaii or in the mountains of Canada?

Would you rather eat live worms or a dead mouse?

Would you rather travel on a train or a plane?

Would you rather watch the news or a movie?

Would you rather be a famous singer or a famous athlete?

Would you rather own a cat or a dog?

Would you rather be a Sumo wrestler or a WWE wrestler?

Would you rather be a potato or a carrot?

Would you rather be an apple or a banana?

Would you rather ride a bike or go swimming?

Would you rather go out for dinner or eat at home?

Dates on the GO!

Special days are especially fun. Breton and Tyler like to make their special days memorable by finding new places to explore and things to do. So here's the plan for Dates on the Go: randomly pick one of the activities listed below. Then just go do it; it's that simple. When you are finished, capture a memory about the cool thing you did by drawing a picture, writing a poem, or jotting some notes in the space on the page. You can also share the experience by posting a photo on social media or by calling a friend and telling them about your day. Special days are as great to share as they are to make.

Ride elevators in the city to find the fastest one, cleanest one, best view, etc.

Go play I Spy in a public place.

Go to the park and swing on the swing set.

Try geocaching.

Go out for tea or coffee and play Coffee Talk.

Get dressed up in each other's clothes (where you can).

Drive around and show off your favorite places.

Go play a sport together.

Dress up and put on a play.

Go out for lunch.

Go outside and do a favorite seasonal activity (build a snow fort, jump in a pile of raked leaves, swim at the beach, etc.)

Go perform a random act of kindness (give away some blankets to homeless people, walk a dog at the SPCA, etc.)

Go for a hike.

Go buy a canvas and some paints, and together paint a masterpiece.

Go for a bike ride or go swimming.

Pick an international recipe that neither of you have made. Cook it together.

Set up a lemonade stand and sell cold drinks on a hot day.

Teach the other person how to do something new.

Play a game of cards.

Let your child pick a board game and play it together.

Kids, teach your parent how to play a video game, or parents, teach your child to play pinball.

Fill up some water balloons and have a water balloon fight.

Drive down streets and pick out the prettiest houses.

Paint a picture of each other.

Take out Lego and build a town.

Visit a local art gallery.

Pull out the "old" photo albums to look at the pictures together.

Go home and clean the house or make dinner together as a surprise for someone special.

Plant a garden together.

Build a fort out of pillows in the living room, and have an indoor campout.

Make a puppet show and perform it for your family or neighbors.

Set up an obstacle course and invite people from your neighborhood to try it out.

Build a campfire in your front yard and have a s'mores stand (like a lemonade   stand).

Visit a local museum.

Write a scavenger hunt list and then go find it. (Better yet, invite a couple of families to join you on the hunt.)

Go "car shopping" and test drive your favorite cars for fun.

Go to a duck pond, feed the ducks, and skip stones.

Make a time capsule, bury it, and make a "treasure map" to find it five years from now.

Parents, write a letter to your child, and kids, write a letter to yourselves for when you get married about things you need to remember or what you are looking for in a partner, or the recipe to fall in love.

Go volunteer together.

Start an exercise program together.

Buy some bags of sand and build a sand castle (or go to the beach and do the same).

Message from Breton & Tyler

Dear Special Day Team:

We are so happy you chose to share a *Coffee Talk: Project Special Day!* We are passionate about helping connect people in meaningful ways by bringing to the world books and activities like this.

As we move forward in publishing this (and other) series of books and games, we need your help to build a community of people with that same loving and authentic desire to create more meaningful relationships worldwide. We ask you to join us and share our work with your extended families, your circles of friends, and your colleagues.

Like us at: www.facebook.com/motivationalkeynote & /teambuildingactivityshop

Buy or share *Coffee Talk:* www.tylerhayden.com or www.teammover.com

Buy or share a book: www.messageinabottlebook.com

Follow us on Twitter: @mybottlebook or @livinlifelarge

Please share the excitement of connecting with others in meaningful ways through your social and professional networks. We look forward to bringing more messages to more people — and with your help, we will make that vision a reality!

Thank you so much for being part of our Special Day.

Breton and Tyler Hayden

www.ingramcontent.com/pod-product-compliance
Lightning Source LLC
Chambersburg PA
CBHW031732210326
41519CB00050B/6309